Designed to SHINE!
Read Aloud Rhymes for Any Size Heart
Volume Two

by Joy Resor
Joy On Your Shoulders
P.O. Box 951
Pisgah Forest, NC 28768

Find Joy on the Web: joyonyourshoulders.com

Copyright © 2021 by Joy On Your Shoulders

Illustrator: Lauren Connell
Book Design: Deborah Dorchak
Creative Consultant: Wendi Kelly

Notice of Rights
All rights reserved. No part of this book may be reproduced or transmitted in any form by any means, electronic, mechanical, photocopying, recording, or otherwise, without the prior written permission of the publisher.

For information on getting permission for reprints and excerpts, contact:
joy@joyonyourshoulders.com.

Softcover ISBN: 978-1-7364587-0-9

Designed to SHINE!
Read Aloud Rhymes for Any Size Heart
Volume Two

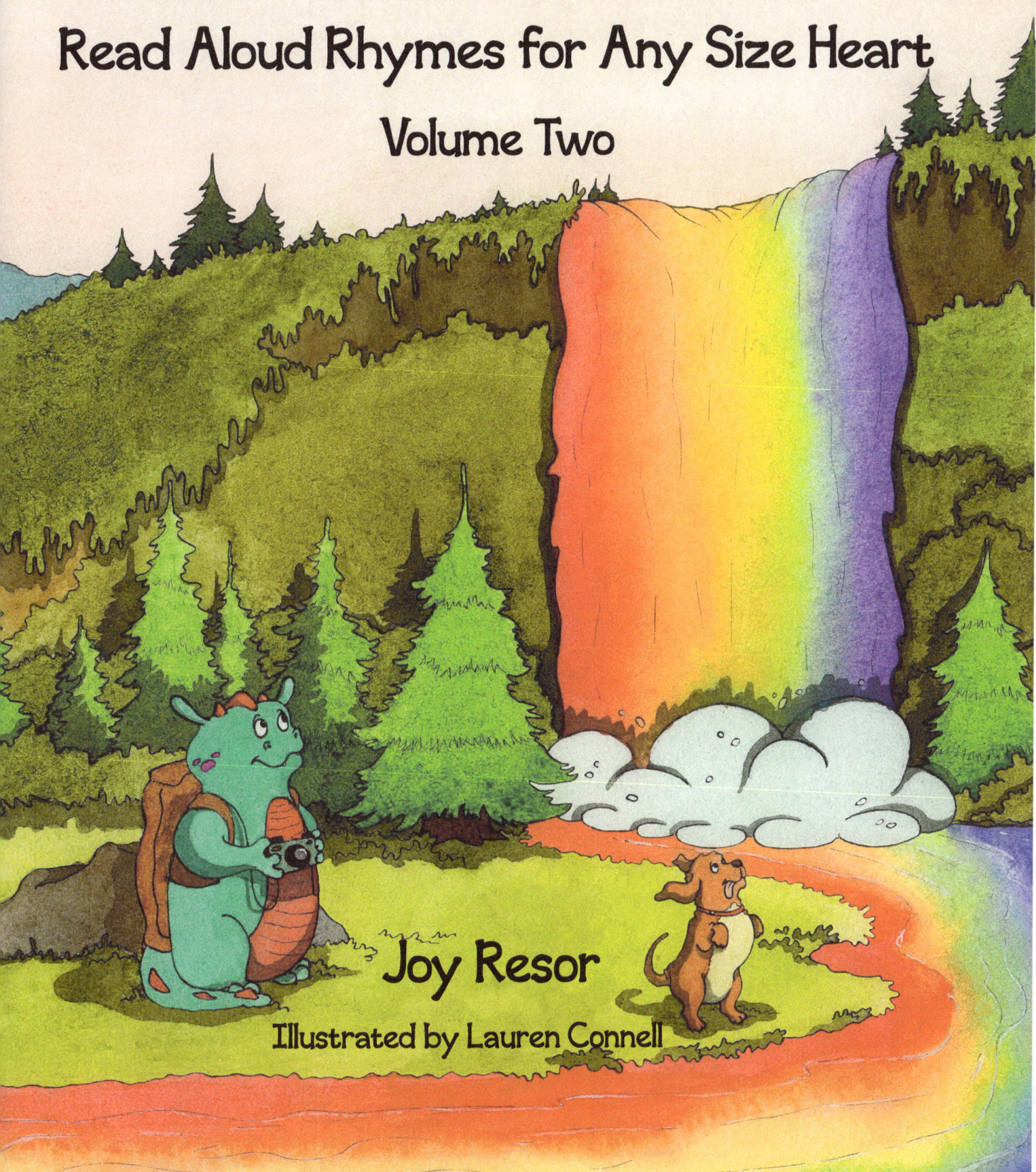

Joy Resor

Illustrated by Lauren Connell

I am so happy you're holding Volume Two of *Designed to SHINE!*

New book owner, when you realize that you love this book, please spread word—write reviews, tell friends and relatives in gatherings and on social media.

There's no right way to savor this book; read a rhyme a day or more.

Rest as you're able or run to the corner; honor your feelings.

Order signed copies through https://www.joyonyourshoulders.com

Drive to any independent bookstore to place orders, supporting them.

Use caution whenever you're on the road.

Consider kindness and compassion to your sweet self.

Tuck in children or grandchildren with warm traditions.

I thank my gifted and talented illustrator Lauren Connell for wondrous artwork, my younger son Kevin Resor for editing suggestions and my partner Michael who supports me in a zillion ways and who listened to the rhymes, offering ideas to consider.

Once again, it's been a complete honor and privilege to allow this book to come through my heart and hands to bless all who receive its fruits.

No Introduction would be complete without thanking book divas Deb Dorchak and Wendi Kelly for being awesome team members...THANK YOU!

Love,

Joy

AMAZING

Today is AMAZING
To breathe and to be!

A day like no other
A day to agree

That this day of all days
Gives you time to AMAZE !

Be wild, be daring
Start a new craze!

How else can you honor
This day of all days?

By sharing a cookie?
By crafting a maze?

This day to AMAZE
In this year of all years

Is yours to treasure
WITH EXTRA LOUD CHEERS !

BELIEVE

BELIEVE in the goodness
Which lives inside you

No matter who says
It's not really true.

You're stardust on earth
With beauty to spare

Created from LOVE
That's meant to be shared.

So lift up your chin
With the light that you shine

As you smile deep inside
Breathing joy, so divine.

BELIEVE in dear YOU!
You are who you are.

Your gifts and your talents
WILL HELP YOU GO FAR!

CREATE

CREATE as you will
Every day if you can.

A song, a poem
A dance with your hands.

What's stirring that asks
To be something new?

A play starring Kris
And his twin kangaroo?

A story 'bout Sergio
Whose left elbow's blue?

CREATE to inspire
Your time past boo hoo.

Spend hours with Sis
When rain gets you down

CREATING new ways
TO TURN 'ROUND A FROWN!

DREAM

Do bears DREAM in dens
Waking groggy in spring?

Do bees DREAM in hives
Of the honey they bring?

Listen to whispers
Which come from your heart.

Honor the DREAMS
You receive in the dark.

DREAMING is fun
As a way that we see

The acorns of life
Growing into tall trees.

No matter which DREAMS
Rat-a-tat upon you

May those that you answer
BRING LIFE THAT IS NEW!

EXTRA

If you could have EXTRA
EXTRA what would you like?

A notebook, a cookie?
Mint ice cream, a hike?

How would it feel –
EXTRA kisses on cheeks

From loved ones who love
All the sweetness you leak?

When super kind you
Skips into your day

Adding light touches
Like kittens at play

You feel EXTRA, a bonus
A gift just for you.

Now hug your sweet self
WITH FEELINGS SO TRUE!

FROSTING

On a day that you top
With FROSTING so bright

How will it look?
Will it shine through the night?

Do you stand on a hill
To watch the sun rise?

Do you pay close attention
With wide open eyes

To a friend who needs you?
To a neighbor who's sad?

Does FROSTING lead you
To giggle a tad?

Invent a new way
For this great day to shake.

Remember that FROSTING
IS NOT JUST FOR CAKE!

GOOFY

Grown-ups, oh Grown-ups
Please settle your minds

From serious ways
You're often inclined.

Lean into GOOFY!
Give silly a try!

How will it look?
Like a grape apple pie?

Would you skip, would you hop
Would you plop on a swing?

Play bells on your way
For the jingle they ring?

How would more GOOFY
Add fun to your day?

Let GOOFY ideas
EXPLODE INTO PLAY!

HURRY

HURRY yourself into
Slowing way down

Since too much of flurry
Can give you a frown.

You could bump into walls
Or stub your big toe

When fast is your pace
Accidents grow.

Give up your HURRY
Add space to your time.

Let daydreams roll into
Eight ways to be kind.

Take a seat on the porch
To slow down your way.

Let breathing bring pause
THIS VERY FINE DAY!

INVITE

INVITE red robins
To sing on your sill

INVITE red roses
To scent as they will.

INVITE drifting clouds
To show you their shapes

As Peter the Panda
Eats apple pancakes.

INVITE tender drops
Of tears on your face

To free all your feelings
Which clears space for grace.

INVITE all the LOVE
That lives in your heart

To light up your life
TODAY IS THE START!

JUGGLE

When clowns toss blue balls
Up high in the air

They JUGGLE with laughter
With smiles, with flare.

You're not in the circus
Your hair's not hot red

Leave JUGGLING to clowns
Let's clean off your bed.

Is your closet too full?
Are your books on the floor?

Does baseball or ballet
Feel like a chore?

What's yours to release
In a jungle of days

When JUGGLING too much
LEAVES NO TIME TO PLAY?

KEY

Grown-ups might tell you
Their KEYS to success

Wisdom they've learned
And ways you should dress.

Listen to KEYS
They lovingly share.

Add lessons you learn
To your unique flare.

You're you, so you
Like pianos we know

With black and white KEYS
Playing music that flows.

A KEY to each life
Is to honor the days.

Your soul speaks inside
IN REMARKABLE WAYS!

LOSE

Did your team LOSE the game?
Did the coach yell and shout?

Did you LOSE a cool toy
When you took a new route?

LOSING'S not fun
But a way life can go.

We gain and we LOSE
It's how days can flow.

Life is in moments
That come as they are

Like finding lost toys
In grandfather's car.

Learn from the gifts
Of LOSSES you face

To feel what you feel
AS TEARS LEAVE THEIR TRACE.

MAIL

Does MAIL in the box
Addressed just to you

Give life to your hope
Of envelopes blue?

Can you write one today?
Would this add to your bliss?

MAIL words from your heart
That you seal with a kiss.

Write a letter to Gram
Stamp MAIL for Aunt Sue

Send photos to sister
At Camp Bugaboo.

MAIL coming from you
Delivers deep care

Since so many Selfies
HAVE MADE LETTERS RARE!

NOW

Three cheers for this moment
The one you're in NOW!

This NOW is amazing
This NOW is KER-POW!

NOW has a message
That you need to know –

NOW moments unfold
Showing up when you grow.

Deeply breathe into
The beautiful view.

Be with it . . . sit down
Watch one bird or two.

The past is behind you
The future's not here

NOW is the time you can
COUNT ON, MY DEAR!

ONE

When you think of ONE
What comes to your mind?

A house, a car or a
ONE of a kind

Griggle Machoo that
Your sister left you?

What about people?
Is separate true?

Has anyone told you
'Bout the ONENESS we are

Connected by LOVE
No matter how far?

That's awesome to me
How's it feel inside you?

Our universe breathes
WITH ONENESS STRAIGHT THROUGH!

PATIENCE

PATIENCE in children
Can rather be missed.

For who wants to wait
For one's lunch to be fixed?

And who has PATIENCE
For birthdays to come

Or parades to begin
With marchers and drums?

Though PATIENCE, my dear
May start out quite small

As you grow and mature
As your height becomes tall

Your PATIENCE will grow
Like trees that reach high.

You'll laugh that to wait
ONCE CAUSED YOU TO CRY!

QUIVER

QUIVER appears when
A scene makes your squirm

Like digging in dirt
Where worms tend to worm.

Like Rover who QUIVERS
On the way to his vet

And how jello jiggles
After it's set.

Getting called on in class
When you'd rather pass

Can turn on a QUIVER
Which zooms in real fast!

Don't sweat if you QUIVER
Don't worry a bit.

It's part of your day
THAT FITS HOW IT FITS!

REST

REST when you're tired
Like after you've run

REST after beach time
Ablaze in the sun.

REST beneath trees
Where birds tweet and nest

Where cool air feels great
When you've run out of zest.

REST on the sofa
With dog's fur to pet

The wag of his tail
Tickling your chest.

Or slip into bed
To close tender eyes

For REST beneath covers
Until the sunrise.

SAVE

SAVE seats at a table
SAVE time as you may

SAVE candy for later
As grown-ups might say.

What will you SAVE?
Count pennies, SAVE dimes?

SAVE spills from the floor?
Memorize rhymes?

Squirrels SAVE their nuts
In the ground or a tree

And Auntie SAVES socks
For crafting with glee.

Does Grandma SAVE china
For a holiday treat?

No SAVING for snowmen
WHO MELT IN THE HEAT!

THANK YOU

THANK YOU, I will
Have a piece of that fruit

And THANKS to the weasel
Who's cuter than cute.

THANK YOU to bro
For the hints that he gives

Of ways to be gentle
And how softness lives.

Give THANKS for the meal
When you sit down to eat

And THANK YOU to friends
Whenever we greet.

THANK YOU, oh sunshine
Who offers us light

And THANK YOU to stars
WHO SHINE THROUGH THE NIGHT!

UP

Raise hands and your head
Awaken your heart

As you lift UP your eyes
A new glow will start.

Like birds UP in trees
See how they sing?

Like clouds floating by
And the joy that they bring.

Now get UP and dance
As you sing to new tunes

Your smile will widen
As your energy blooms.

It expands, you expand
While you live into more

More happy, more zip
IT'S YOURS TO EXPLORE!

VOICE

Can your VOICE find a way
Like seeds that are sown

To speak in a VOICE
That's truly your own?

Without super loudness,
Whining or tears

May your VOICE land in place
To speak beyond fear.

Express what's inside
For it does matter so

May your VOICE speak right out
With wisdom you know.

With whispers, with quiet
A VOICE can find ways

To light a clear path
FOR ANYONE'S DAYS!

WHERE

WHERE do you shimmer?
While climbing a tree?

Running through puddles
Or sitting to be?

WHERE are the flowers
That smell so divine

Adding fragrance to gardens
With beauty so fine?

WHERE is the cozy
Dear you likes to seek?

In bed? On the couch?
On the grass? By a creek?

WHERE is the smile
That warms up your face?

WHERE else can you shine
ADDING LIGHT TO A SPACE?

XEROX

XEROX means copy
If you didn't yet know

And how would it feel
To XEROX the snow?

Would you make a huge pile?
Would you tunnel on through?

Would you XEROX your pet
Turning one fish to two?

Would you XEROX a dream
Of castles near seas

Or XEROX an owl
Who lives in tall trees?

And what about LOVE?
Let's XEROX it please

So LOVE will surround
OUR WORLD ON THE BREEZE!

YELLOW

YELLOW's a color
To make your heart sing.

Lemons, Bananas.
Your radiance, your zing!

The brightness of sunshine
The color of crayons

Roses in vases
Corn kernels in cans.

Let YELLOW delight you
As much as it will

With rainbows of joy
Meeting daisies on hills.

Wear YELLOW in rain
To brighten the tone.

If you want to taste snow
LEAVE YELLOW ALONE!

ZEAL

ZEAL means passion and
Big interest, too.

What makes you excited?
What gives you a clue?

Do zip lines bring ZEAL
Or sledding down hills?

What lights you right up?
What thrills give you chills?

Are you ZEALOUS for cats
Or roosters at dawn?

ZEALOUS for bikes or
A doe with her fawn?

Crazy Hat Pat?
Dressing up like a seal?

List 25 ways
TO LIVE INTO ZEAL!

Additional Books by Joy Resor

Go In Joy! An Alphabetical Adventure

Go In Joy! An Alphabetical Adventure Second Edition

Go In Joy! Venture to Your Center
—Journaling Prompts to Enliven Your Joy

Designed to SHINE! Read Aloud Rhymes for Any Size Heart

Signed books are available through
https://www.joyonyourshoulders.com

Unsigned books are available at any independent bookstore and online.

ABOUT THE AUTHOR

Joy Resor shines in western North Carolina where she writes books that inspire readers, serves clients as their spiritual mentor and loves sharing life with her partner Michael. Daily grateful for all that life brings, Joy leans into adventures that call to her soul. She looks forward to visits with her grown sons and their wives and to reading with grandchildren.

joyonyourshoulders.com

ABOUT the ILLUSTRATOR

Lauren Connell is an artist who loves to illustrate the whimsical world around her. She works in a multitude of mediums, from watercolor to printmaking. She lives in North Georgia with her farm animals and family, hiking and traveling whenever she can. The outdoors are a great influence on her work and keep her inspired.

www.ingramcontent.com/pod-product-compliance
Lightning Source LLC
Chambersburg PA
CBHW042254100526
44589CB00002B/16